# THE RIDICULOUSLY SIMPLE GUIDE TO GOOGLE HOME HUB

## A PRACTICAL GUIDE TO SETTING UP A SMART HOME

PHIL SHARP

Ridiculously Simple Press
ANAHEIM, CALIFORNIA

# Contents

# INTRODUCTION

In 2016, Google announced it was getting into the home assistant business with Google Home. The smart device allowed users to essentially have a computer controlled by their voice. Google was just getting started. In 2017, Google released two more devices: the Google Home Mini and Google Home Max.

Finally, in 2018, Google announced that its smart speaker would get a whole lot more visual with the Google Home Hub.

The Google Home Hub is a hybrid of two worlds--a device that works best with both your voice and by touch. The same voice commands as the non-touch Google Home's are there, but a screen gives it the extra touch you need to control things in your home like security cameras.

It's original, powerful, and just a little weird! It's unlike anything you've ever used--not quite a tablet, not quite a voice assistant, not quite a computer--it's a Hub!

Because it's a little weird, it takes some getting used to; this guide will walk you through what you need to know to get the most out of the powerful display.

Ready to get started?!

# [1]

# TELL ME THE BASICS...AND KEEP IT RIDICULOUSLY SIMPLE!

This chapter will cover:
- What separates the Google Home Hub from other smart home devices.
- A tour of the main components.

## How It Compares

Chances are, if you are considering the Google Home Hub, then you've heard about the Echo and Portal--and also some of the other Google smart hub devices like Lenovo.

|  | Google Home Hub | Echo Show |
|---|---|---|
|  |  |  |

| Price | $149 | $229 |
|---|---|---|
| Connectivity | Wi-Fi, Bluetooth | Wi-Fi, Bluetooth |
| Camera | Not supported | 5 MP |
| Weight | 480g | 1,775g |
| Dimensions | 178.5 x 118 x 67.3 | 246 x 174 x 107 |
| Voice Assistant | Google Assistant | Alexa |
| YouTube Support | Yes | Not natively |
| Multi-room Audio | Yes | Yes |

In the end, the choice is obviously yours, but most people go with the ecosystem they are most invested in. If you already have Echo's in your house and are a Kindle power user, then the Echo Show makes sense. Facebook makes sense if you want the most power and camera, and absolutely adore the social network.

One caveat about any Amazon device, however, can be summed up in a word: YouTube. Amazon devices do not currently support YouTube. This can be a gamechanger for users who really want the device in the kitchen to watch cooking videos. There are workarounds, but they aren't ideal for novice users.

## The Ridiculously Simple Tour

In the next chapter, I'll go over how to get things set up; before that, however, it's helpful to have a brief tour of the Google Home Hub, so you know what to expect once you have things up and running.

The Google Home Hub may look like a tablet, but don't be mistaken. This isn't the full-feature tablet you may be used to. There are no shortcut menus or even an App Store. It's all very basic, and that's the point. The goal of the device is for someone to be able to master it quickly.

In this chapter, I'll cover the navigation and main areas of the device, but it's purposely short because there aren't a lot of them to cover.

My apologies for some of the images in the book-- unlike typical devices that have screenshot or device recording, the Google Home Hub does not have this feature natively; photos here were captured the old fashion way: with a camera.

### Main Display

The main display can't be configured. Don't spend time trying to add a wallpaper because you simply cannot do it.

It displays the time on the left and the currently open app on the right. By default, it's the calendar, but if you have or had Spotify open, then it would have that instead.

You can see the forecast for any particular day, by tapping on the day. It brings up the weather screen for that, and then on the bottom will give you the option to see other days. You can also scroll through the weather hour-by-hour, by sliding your finger over the hourly weather.

To get back to the main screen, swipe right from the left edge; you can also wait about ten seconds, and it will automatically go back to the screen.

Whatever is displayed on the right side, can also be tapped; this launched the app in full screen. In this example, it is my calendar.

Getting back to the main screen is always the same: swipe right from the left edge of the device.

You can't get rid of what's displayed on the right, so don't try and force close the app. Open a new app and it's automatically replaces.

## Swipe Up

Swipe up from the lower bottom of the screen to get your device controls. There's only two: on the left is the volume (which can also be managed with the physical toggles on the back of the device) and screen brightness (on the right).

To the far right is a config control gear; if you tap this, you'll get a menu with a few options.

It's not like a typical config menu that's loaded with things you can configure. There's really very little you can do hear. On the top is the Wi-Fi (which you have to change on the app, so it's really just a, "hey this is the Wi-Fi you are using"--not very helpful, right?), below this is the "About device" menu, which, again, doesn't do anything--it's just information about your device.

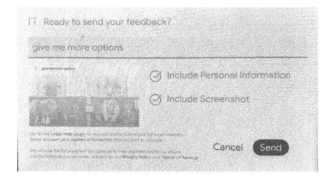

Finally, the bottom option is to send feedback. This is the only option that lets you actually do anything. You can, you guessed it, send feedback! This option will ask you what's wrong, and you dictate (no keyboards are on the device) what the problem is, and then you'll have the option to send it with a screenshot. You more than likely will not hear back from Google, so don't use this to ask for help.

## Swipe Down

Swipe down from the top and you'll get the "Welcome home" menu. This is where all your connected devices have shortcuts.

You, unfortunately, can't manually add shortcuts or move around the ones that are already there. If it's not clear yet: the Google Hub Home is a very stripped down and basic device. The goal is to give you quick access to your connected home--not to use it for productivity as you would any other tablet-like device.

Tapping on view rooms will show you all the rooms that have connected devices. If you only have a Google Home Hub, then this will look pretty bare. All the devices you see can be touched, but many are very limited in features. Some do nothing at all, such as the example below.

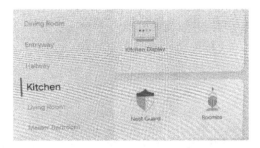

You can control them with your voice, but that's it. The options in the Welcome home menu should be pretty self-explanatory--except for one: broadcast. Broadcast is a very cool little feature if you have several Google Home's; broadcast will "broadcast" a message to every connected Google Home in your house. So you can say "Dinners ready" and throughout your house, everyone will get the message. You can also do this from your Google Home by saying, "Hey Google, broadcast: INSERT MESSAGE HERE."

**Swipe Left**

Swipe left from the far right of your screen to get a series of screens with recommendations.

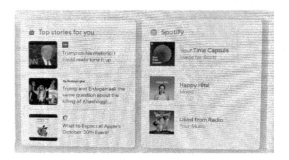

Here you'll see a playlist of videos, music, and suggestions for more things you can do with the device.

The more it gets to know you, the better the suggestions get.

# [2]
# CONNECTING YOUR HOME
# TO THE GOOGLE HOME HUB

This chapter will cover:
- Setting up the Google Home Hub.
- Connecting your smart devices to the Google Home Hub.

## Getting Started

One thing you'll notice pretty quick is there are no power buttons on the Google Home Hub. In fact, there are only two buttons total: the volume button and the mic on / off.

So how do you turn it on? Plug it in. That's it. The Home Hub is always on so there's no need turn it on or off. That means if you want it off you have to pull the power cord. If you are worried about energy, this is an energy efficient device, so leaving it on 24/7 won't drive up your energy bill.

Once you plug in the Google Home Hub, you'll see a loading screen; in a few seconds, the setup screen will appear. It says: Get the app.

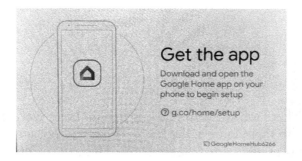

You read that right! Unlike the setup, you might be used to on phones and tablets, the setup on the Google Home Hub requires an app on your phone. You'll see why this is important later in the book. For now, just go to the app store on your tablet or phone and download the Google Home app.

*NOTE: If you already have a Google Home device in your home, then you already have the app. All Google Home devices are setup and run in the same app.*

From the Google app, tap "Add".

There are a few things you can do here; we'll come back to them later in the book. What's important in this step is to add your Google Home Hub, so select "Add Device".

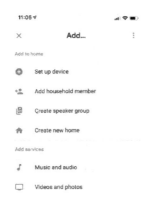

Next, you can add a Google device or another smart device. In this step, you'll want to add the Google Home Hub, so tap: "Set up new devices".

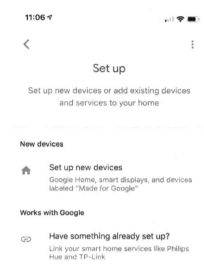

You can have several different home networks--so you could control your main house and, for instance, a rental home. If you don't have any, then select "Create another home".

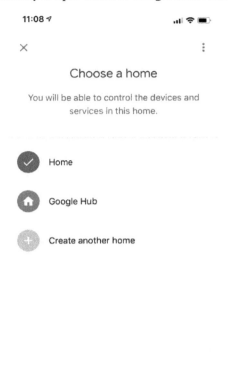

It will ask you to give it a nickname; this can be whatever you like. Some sort of identifier is what I recommend (such as "vacation home").

If you already have your network set up from previous devices, then just select it and tap Next.

It will automatically start looking for devices.

In just a few seconds, it will recognize your Google Home Hub and come back with a screen that displays the name.

Tap the Google Home Hub, and select "Next". It will now automatically add and configure the device.

In just a few seconds, a code will display on both your Google Home Hub and in your app. Confirm that the code is the same on both devices, and then hit "Yes". If they're different, then select "No".

The next screen asks your permission to share stats and crashes with Google (you'll also note at this point, the Google Home Hub has returned to the "Get the app" screen--that's okay, it will change when you finish the setup on your phone).

What this screen is asking you is if you want to help Google make the device even better; it won't be able to see sensitive things like email--it just sends them a crash report that says, "hey, when x user did y, z happened." If you don't want to share this, then select "NO THANKS". It's all optional and doesn't change the Google Home Hub experience.

The next step is telling Google where you will put the device. This doesn't change anything on the device itself-

-like it won't work different if you select living room vs. kitchen. It's just to help the app identify and organize your devices. Tap where it will go, or scroll to the bottom to add a custom room. Then tap next.

Next, you'll add your wifi to the device. Select the network strongest in the room you are putting the device and hit next. You won't have to add your wifi password if you've added it on your phone. It's all seamlessly added.

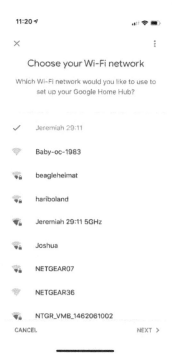

The bread and button of the Google Home Hub (and Google Home in general) is Google Assistant. This is the assistant you speak to when you ask Google a question like "What's the weather?" The next portion of the setup will cover this.

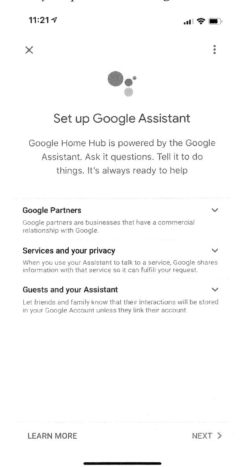

Next, you'll teach Google your voice. It's surprisingly sophisticated and can tell when you are speaking vs. someone else in the house. So when you say "Ok, Google: what's on my calendar" you'll get different results than when your spouse says it. Read the tutorial, then select "I agree" unless you don't want this feature, in which case you would select "No thanks".

11:22 ⏴                              ⋯ 🛜 🔋

### Teach your Assistant to recognize your voice

Voice Match helps your Assistant identify your voice and tell you apart from others by creating a unique model of your voice on this device.

**Why set up Voice Match?** It allows multiple users to enroll on this device. You can also use your voice to access personal results, which you can turn on after setting up Voice Match.

**Keep in mind:** A similar voice or recording might be able to access your personal results, too. You can

NO THANKS                    VIEW MORE ›

---

It will ask you to say a few things--unless you've already set this up with your other Google Home devices. If that's the case then you're already setup! You'll have another setup screen that you have to agree to.

## Get personal results with your voice

Voice Match has been set up.

Now you can turn on personal results to use your voice to access your calendar, contacts, reminders and more on this device. Learn more

Personal results, plus personalized YouTube video recommendations, can also appear – without you having to ask for them – on the Home screen and as notifications. Note that curious bystanders can also tap and act on these results.

You can turn off personal results in Assistant settings.

NO THANKS                    VIEW MORE

Now it's time to decide what Google Home Hub sounds like. You can hear each of them by selecting "Play sample". Voice 1 is a female and Voice 2 is a male. Select on and select "Next".

The next step is adding your address. This step is optional but will help you if you will be using location-based apps like traffic and weather.

Adding media services will be done in the next step. You probably got a multi-month trial to YouTube and other services with the device. You can deselect them if you don't want them.

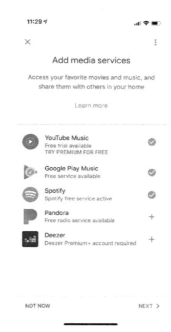

If you have other digital media services (like HBO Now) you can add it in the next screen.

Next, is something Google calls Duo. This toggles your phone number to the Google Home Hub so you can make and receive calls from your device. Like many things in the setup, it's optional and can be removed later.

## Duo calling

Use your existing Duo account for audio calls
on your Smart Display. Your friends and
family can reach you at +1 714-404-7182

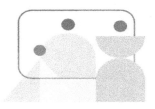

You can unlink your Duo account from this device any
time in Assistant settings.

NOT NOW                                    USE DUO >

If you decide to use Duo, then the next screen will ask if you also want to add contacts. This is optional but will make it more personal. So, for instance, if you are getting a call from your dad, it will say "Dad's calling" vs. just displaying a number.

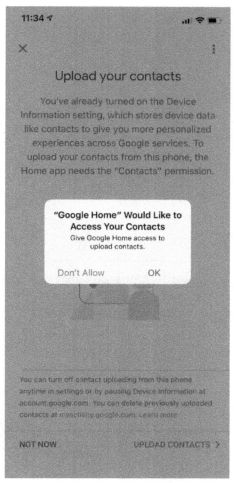

What displays on your standby screen (i.e. when the screen is idle) is what you decide next. You have three options: Google Photos (which means it will show photos that are sync'd to your Google Photos account), Art Gallery (famous art work), or an old fashion clock.

Each one has different views that you can display.

After hitting next, you get the Almost Done screen. This is where you can add a payment (and get one final chance to change settings before finishing--and remember by final, I don't mean final! You can change them later!).

Why would you want to add a payment? If you want to say something like "Ok, Google: order me a pizza" it will be able to bill your card so you don't have to do anything later. It's all optional.

Once you tap next, your display will be ready to go! Just select "Continue."

11:38 ✓                                       ⬤

✕                                             ⋮

Kitchen Display is ready

Now let's explore what you can do

CONTINUE >

Okay, I spoke too soon! You'll see that next screen shows the setup actually isn't finished--sort of! Yeah, it's confusing right! The setup is actually done, and if you go to your Google Home Hub, you can now select finish setup.

So, what's up with these screens? They're more tutorials than setup screens.

The next screens will adjust the Ambient EQ light sensor. What's that? When things are bright it will show your Photos or whatever you have selected; when things go dark it automatically dims and turns on the clock.

## Ambient EQ light sensor

This automatically adjusts the screen
brightness to blend into the room. And nope,
it's not a camera.

NEXT >

---

    The next screen tells you that your Google Home Hub
has a mic toggle--like I said: it's a tutorial not a setup at
this point. It's just telling you that if you don't want
Google to listen to your commands, then just switch it off.

Volume is the next screen. Up to increase it. Down to decrease it. Not a lot to this, right?!

Finally, you'll see more things you can buy. Once you are done looking at this screen, go to the Google Home Hub and select: Finish setup.

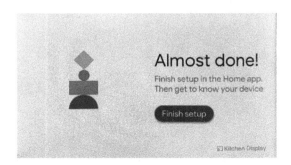

Now a video will play. Unfortunately, you can't skip it, but you can turn the volume down and ignore it. It goes for about a minute. It will only play once.

When the video is over, you'll have to swipe right once when prompted.

You are now ready to go! The main menu will appear.

## Adding Your Home

Once you are set up, you're ready to get set up!

Confused? Don't worry: this is all painless! The next step is adding your smart devices to your Google Home Hub. You might not have any yet. If not, that's ok. There's still plenty you can do.

For this book, I'll show you how to add a Nest. Nest is a smart home device that includes everything from Smart doorbells to smoke alarms.

Like many Smart home devices, you can add it right to the Google Home Hub.

To get started go to your Google Home app on your phone or tablet.

If it's not on the main screen, then go to the bottom menu tabs, and tap on the little house.

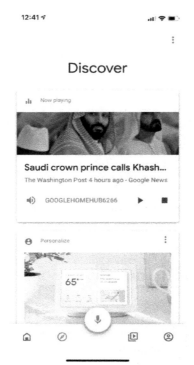

Next, select Add.

# Home ▾

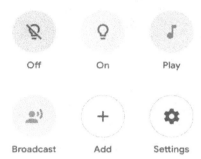

| Off | On | Play |
| --- | --- | --- |

| Broadcast | Add | Settings |
| --- | --- | --- |

You'll be setting up a device, so select "Set up device".

For the next step, since Nest is a "Works with Google" device and not "Made with Google" then you'll select the bottom option. You can see what the device is on the box when you buy it--there's usually a sticker that identifies it.

You'll have a lot of options to pick from. All the things you see are supported on the Google Home Hub! I'll scroll until I find the next.

Next I'll need to sign into my Nest account.

Next, it will tell me all the things it can do. I can read through it and then finally hit allow. NOTE: this will look different on each device you add.

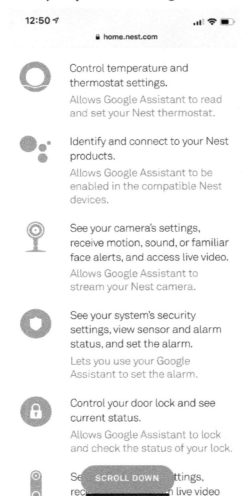

Once it's linked, it will give you a message, then go back to the main screen. The bottoms on top will now include Nest.

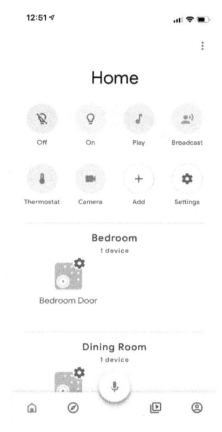

If you go back to your Google Home Hub, you won't see these options right away, but after a few seconds it will sync.

Sometimes what you add will be controlled by voice, but there's no visual UI--in Nest case, at this writing, you cannot see your Home Alarm System, but you can activate it. You can, however, control your Nest thermostat and Nest cameras.

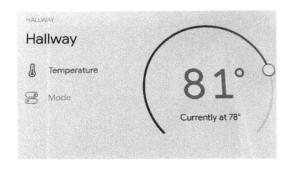

# [3]

# WHAT CAN THIS THING DO?

This chapter will cover:
- Playing iTunes
- Playing Netflix and other media
- Using Google Assistant

## Playing iTunes On the Google Home Hub

The Google Home Hub is, as the name suggests, a Google device! As such, Google would love nothing more for you to use their services to stream music. This means that if you have Apple Music, then you are not going to be able to listen to your music right off the bat.

That doesn't mean you are out of luck. You can still listen to Apple Music. It takes a minute to set up, but it's easy and once it's done, it is easy to keep listening to music each time you come back to the device.

*NOTE: This same method can also be done on Google Home speakers.*

To get started, go to your Google Home app.

Next, tap your device and tap the "Settings" configure button in the upper right corner.

Next, scroll down a bit until you see "Paired Bluetooth devices."

Finally, tap "Enabled Pairing Mode."

Now go into your photos Settings, and select Bluetooth.

Under other settings, you'll see your Google Home Hub (it won't be called Google Home Hub--it will have the name of your device--such as Kitchen Hub). Tap that.

Now go to Apple Music. Play your music. On the bottom center of the app is a triangle with a circle around it. Tap that.

**Atlas Hands**
Benjamin Francis Leftwich — Last S

This will bring up all the devices you can stream music to. Your Google Home Hub will now show up.

Once you tap it, the music will automatically stream to your Google Home Hub.

## Streaming HBO and Netflix

Just like Apple Music, you'll probably want to jump into your Netflix and HBO library and start watching movies on your device, right? Wrong! That's another thing the Google Home Hub won't do natively.

You can, of course, pay for YouTube's paid streaming service and get plenty of movies, but not everyone wants that. And even if you do, chances are, you'll probably want to watch Netflix and HBO (or CBS or Hulu or any number of streaming apps) on your device, right?

Fortunately, while there isn't a native way to watch streaming movies, there is still away.

You'll want to follow the same instructions I give for Apple Music above. If you've already done this, then you are all set!

The next step is jumping into your streaming app, finding what you want to play, and then tapping on the casting option (usually in the upper or bottom corner).

It's not exactly the easy way you may be used to, and it's not like you can say "Ok Google, play Game of Thrones"--although, HBO Now is one of the apps you are able to link, which makes it a little easier.

As time goes, you probably will start seeing the ability to play "some" apps natively through Google Home Hub. This likely will never include Apple Music, but you never no.

## YouTube

YouTube doesn't have a lot of features. When you tap a video that's playing, you can pause it or tap the flag to report it as inappropriate.

After you tap a video, you can swipe up and get the "Up next" view; this shows you the videos that will play after the one that's currently playing if you don't' stop it.

To find other videos, you just say "Ok Google, show me INSERT VIDEO."

## Spotify

Like Google, Spotify is also very basic. You can pause and skip music. That's it!

This is not the full feature app you may be used to. You can get most of the features, but you have to do so with your voice. For example, if you say "Ok Google, show me my playlists" it will bring up a list of all your playlist.

You can also add new music to the playlist, but telling Google to do it--make sure and specify which one.

## Google Assistant

The Google Assistant is the bread and button of Google Home Hub. Because of that, it's going to be helpful to know the commands that bring it to life.

As I've said several times, the Google Home Hub isn't a tablet--but that doesn't mean it doesn't have powerful apps built into it...you just don't see them. There is no calculator app, for instance, but you can still use Google Assistant to get all the same calculations as a calculator. To help get you started, here are the commands you should know about.

This list is in no way comprehensive. There are literally 1000s of Google commands, so have fun asking Google whatever you want to know and see how many things it can tell you!

Just remember to make any of the commands that follow work, you have to say "Ok Google."

### Play Music

I've shown you how you can use the Spotify playlist and play songs. You can also tell Google to play something thematic. Like: play music for a party.

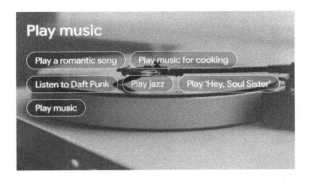

## Check Weather

You should know by now that you can ask Google about the weather, but you can also say things like "do I need an umbrella today" or "what's the UV index" or even "what's the weather in Russia."

## Set Alarms

There is, unfortunately, no way to see all your alarms in an app; that would be helpful. But you can ask Google to show you all your alarms; you can also say things like "wake me up in four hours", "set alarm for twenty minutes from now" or "set alarm for weekdays at 6pm".

## Set Timers

Google can set alarms and times. It works the same way as alarms. And just like alarms, you can say "Cancel all timers" to get rid of everything.

## Reminders

Google has a better memory than you or I! You can use Google Assistant to remember things for me. Like "remind me on Tuesdays at 7 to take out the trash." You can see all of your reminders by saying "show me my reminders."

You can also say "Remember my wife's birthday" and it will ask when it is and remember the date and remind you when it comes up.

## Play Videos

You can ask Google to play you videos like "Play me Michael Jackson music videos" or you can ask for themes like "show me funny videos" or "show me videos that will inspire me". You can also ask for "recommended videos."

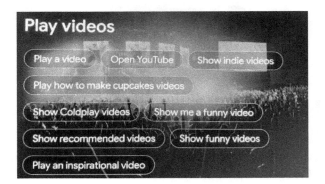

## Recipes

No matter what you want to make, Google can probably find it. Just say "show me gluten-free brownie recipes," "paleo pizza recipes," or even "how many calories are in tacos."

## Manage Photos

Google Photos has gotten pretty smart over the years. It doesn't just recognize faces, it also recognizes places and things. So you can say "show me pictures of my wife," "show me pictures with flowers," or "birthday photos."

## Check Dictionary

Stumped for what a word means? Ask Google! You can ask it to "define it" or just say "what does this word mean."

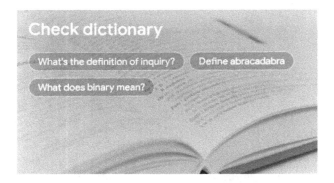

## Make Phone Calls

When setup with your phone, you can make phone calls. Just say who you want to call--like "call dad" or say the number.

## Manage Calendar

You can manage your calendar in the calendar app or just say what you want to do. Like "add doctors appointment to November 3 at 3" or "What's on my calendar this week.

## Control Lighting

Assuming you have smart lights in your home, you can say "turn off the hallway lights' or "are the lights off in the kid's room?"

## Play Audiobooks

Google doesn't let you read books, but it does let you listen to them. If you've purchased a book in the Play store, you can ask Google to play them.

## Time

Google obviously can tell you what time it is, but it also can tell you things about the day, like "what time will the sunset?"

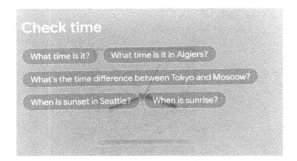

## Convert Units

If you are using the Google Home Hub to cook, then you'll probably want to convert things. You can ask Google "how many kilo is in a pound" or you can ask "how many inches are in a foot." It will convert just about anything!

## Calculator

As mentioned earlier, you can use Google Assistant as a calculator.

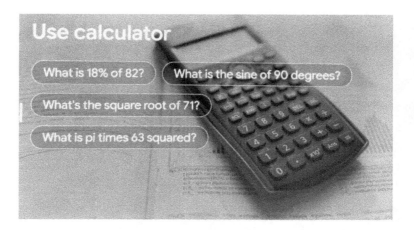

## Translate

Google is sort of the Tower of Babel: It knows all languages! You can ask it to say something in several different languages.

### Find food and drink

Not sure what to eat? Let Google help! Ask "What restaurants are open near me?" You can also specify the kind of restaurant.

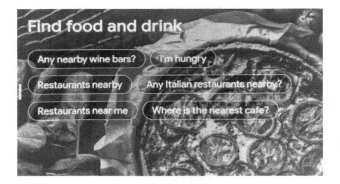

### Nutrition Facts

Worried about calories? Ask Google! How many calories are in an apple? How much fat is in an egg? How much vitamin C is in an orange?

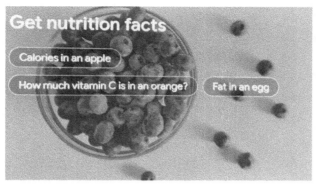

## Control TV

If you have a Chromecast, you can use your Google Assistant to control it. Just make sure and add the Chromecast to your Google Home app.

## Check News

Google is bigger than a newspaper. It's sort of like all the newspapers in one! So you can say "what's in the local news," or "what's in the local news in Paris." You can also ask for particular kinds of news like Sports, Entertainment news, or Political news.

## Check Traffic

Google doesn't have a built-in map, but it can check traffic for you. You can ask "how long will it take to get to work?" Or "how busy is the 5 freeway?"

## Facts

Ask Google about any fact you want to know and you'll probably get an answer. "What's the lifespan of a tiger?" "How fast is a coyote." You'll be amazed at what it knows!

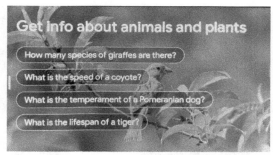

## Finance

Are you a finance person? So is Google! Ask about what a stock is trading at or ask about an entire stock index.

## Date Night

Want to go to the movies? Ask Google when any movie is playing and where. It will find out.

## Weird Google

There was a lot of matter of fact commands in this chapter. Let's end on a lighter note. Here are some sillier things you can ask Google...and get an answer!

- Are we in the Matrix
- Can you pass the Turing test
- I am your father
- Do you speak Morse Code
- Where's Waldo
- Who Let the dogs out
- Who is the real Slim Shady
- Have you seen Bigfoot
- Do you know the Muffin Man
- Do you want to be human?
- What am I thinking right now
- Are you Skynet?
- Tell me something funny
- Talk dirty to me
- Are you married?
- Are you afraid of something?
- What are the three laws of robotics
- Give me a random number
- Beatbox

- What is the meaning of life?

# [4]
# PERSONALIZE YOUR EXPERIENCE

This chapter will cover:
- Changing your settings.
- Changing Your Screen Saver
- Routines
- Personal Settings
- Factory Reset

## Changing the Settings

Now that you know your way around, what if you want to change something? That's all done in the Google Home app from your mobile device.

Let's look at the Device Settings first. To get there, open up your Google Home app.

Next, tap your device.

And finally, tap the configure button in the upper right corner of the app.

This brings up four different setting groups:

- General settings
- Sound settings
- Device settings
- Learn more

## General settings

The general settings is where you change things like the device name (for instance if you want it be called "Awesome Sauce Kitchen" instead of just "Kitchen"), where the device is located (for instance, you move it from the living room to the bedroom), associated Google account, and Wi-Fi.

To change any of these settings, just tap on them. This will bring up a new screen. Once you save it it's all set. After changing a setting, it can take a few minutes to sync to your device. If it never shows up, as a last resort, unplug and plug back in the device.

## Sound settings

The Google Home Hub isn't exactly a killer sound system. Because of that, there's not a lot you can change.

The only main things you can change here is Bass and treble. Just tap the option to bring it up. Once you change it and tap back, it's saved. Give it a few minutes to sync to your device.

## Device settings

You can change the way the device behaves in "Device settings."

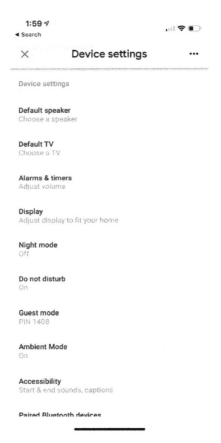

Some of the things you can change:
- Default speaker - if you want sound running through the Google Home Mini instead (assuming you have one)
- Do not disturb - a good setting to have on if the device is in the bedroom, so you don't get alerts while you sleep

- Accessibility - if you need captions on or different lights / sounds because you are visually or hearing impaired.
- Display - this is where you can adjust how soon the screen times out, set brightness, turn on color matching and low light activation, and more.

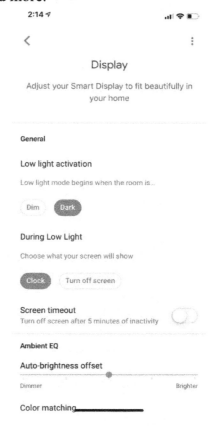

## Learn More

Learn more sounds like some kind of help guide. It's not! It's just a really bad name. Learn more is actually where you can toggle if other can cast to your device and if you want to help improve the device by sharing crashes with Google. Blue means it's toggled on and white means it's toggled off. The last option is to remove the device, which I'll cover next.

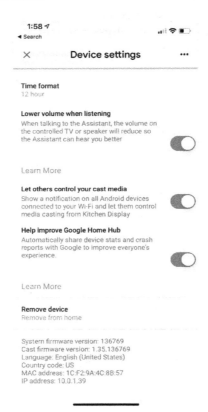

## Who is the artist?

If your device background is set to art, you may want to know more about the artist or work. You can read about it, by going to the Google Home app and tapping on the device. It will show you who is currently on your screen and also let you go to the previous and next art that will or has been displayed.

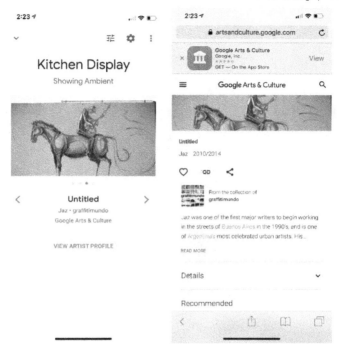

If you tap on that image, it will bring up more information about the work.

## Change Screensaver

Google could have made it a little easier to change the screensaver; at the very least, they could have called it a screensaver! To change it you have to go into the "Ambient settings." Not exactly the word you are looking for to change that setting is it?!

Where is that setting? Go to the Google Home app, then select your device, tap on the configure button in the upper right corner, and then select Ambient mode under "Device settings." From here you can select what you want to appear as a screensaver.

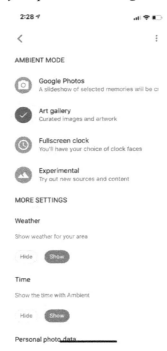

You can also change if you want the time / weather to display and how soon before it goes into screensaver mode.

## Add Another Person to your account

If you have multiple people in your house, you can add them each to your device; that way it's personalized to each person preferences. To do this open the Google Home app, tap add, then add household member. Next, type in their Google Account email address.

## Routines

One relatively new feature to Google is "routines." Routines make it easy to tell your device to do something every day. For instance, you can tell your device to turn on the alarm at a certain time every day or every other day.

To set up routines, go to the Google Home app, tap the account button in the lower right corner

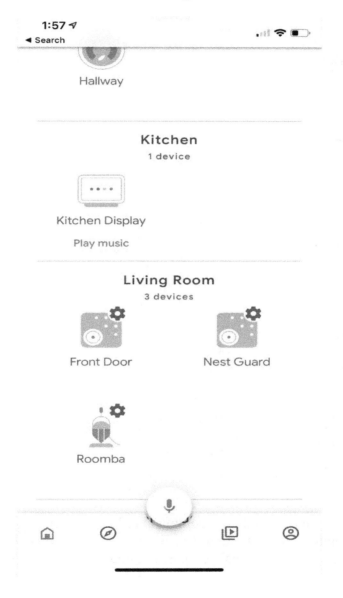

Then settings, and then scroll to the bottom and tap more settings. From here, tap the Assistant tab.

Next, tap routines.

To add a routine, tap the blue plus sign in the lower right corner.

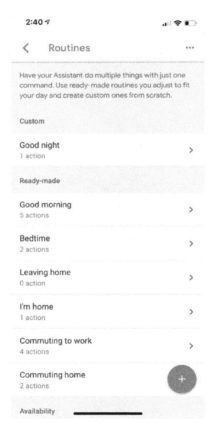

Finally, add your command (when you say....) and optionally the time of day. After you add those, add your action below. Finally, tap Save in the upper right corner.

## Personal settings

You saw how easy it was to add routines. You probably noticed a lot of other settings as you were going through this step. The point of this book is to make things Ridiculously Simple, so I won't over complicate things by going into each one.

I will, however, point out that there's a lot here that you could change--and it's all tied to your Google Account--not the device. So add or changing something here will change it across all devices.

A few things you can change by tapping the account button in the lower right corner, then settings, and then scroll to the bottom and tap more settings:

- The Google Assistants voice
- Your voice match
- Language spoken
- Services connected (such as Spotify or HBO)
- Voice and video calls
- News services
- Photos

## Factory Rest / Turn Off

As noted already, you cannot turn off the device. The only way to do this is to cut power to the device. You won't lose any of your settings doing this if you really want it off.

You can, however, do a factory reset on the device. This restores everything to the original settings and you have to set it up again. This is what you want to do, for example, if you are giving the device to someone else--so your settings are no longer on it.

To do a Factory Reset, hold the volume buttons down (button lower and increase); a message will pop up saying it will do a Factory Reset in 10 seconds. If it's really what you want to do (and remember everything will be lost), then wait for it to finish counting down

The last step is going into your Google Home app on your mobile device, and tapping on the device, then clicking on the configure button in the upper right corner. This brings up the device settings. Scroll to the bottom. The last step is to remove the device.

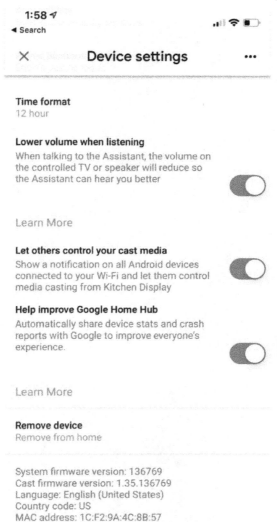

If you need to restart your device, you can do it in the Device settings, and then tapping in the upper right corner on the three dots. This brings up a menu with one option being reboot.

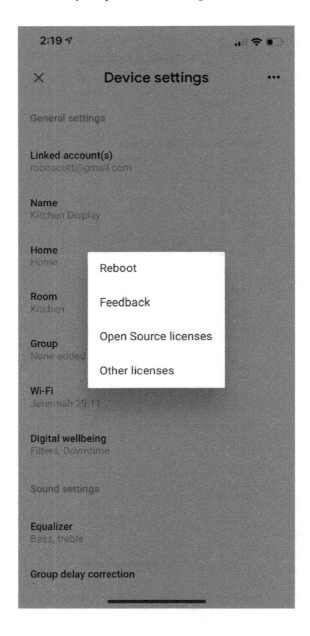

# [5]

# BEST SMART DEVICES FOR GOOGLE HOME HUB

This chapter will cover:
- Best Smart devices you can get for Google Home Hub

So, I've talked a lot about how Apple Music and Netflix only "sort of" work in Google Home Hub, and how you'll find a lot of devices behave the same. So, did you pay for a pretty picture frame or does thing actually do something?!

While there are obviously a few things not quite compatible with the Google Home Hub, there are plenty of more that are compatible. In this chapter, I'll go over a few of them so if you are interested in setting up your home with smart devices you'll know what to look for.

**Nest**

When it comes to Smart devices, the best bang for your buck in terms of what works with Google Home Hub is Nest. Nest was purchased by Google several years back, so obviously Google want so to make all it's products compatible.

Nest has a thermostat, lock, doorbell, smoke alarm, security camera, security alarm--in other words, you can pretty much connect your entire home with Nest products. Here's the problem: it's several thousand dollars to buy everything for every room!

What my house does--and what a lot of houses do--is have a mixture of Nest and non-Nest devices. We, for instance, use the Nest thermostat and security cameras, but we don't use the doorbell camera.

If you can afford it, then you won't dislike it. But if you are like most people, it's too much of an investment. Fortunately, there are lots of other products that do the same thing only cheaper.

## Thermostat

Nest is one of the industry leader in the Smart home space, but right next to it is Honeywell. Honeywell has been making non-smart devices for years.

The Honeywell RTH9585WF is one of their newest models and it is compatible with Google.

## Lighting

The most know lighting system for Smart homes is the Philips Hue light. The problem is, it's a little pricey.

I use the Geeni bulb in my house. It's compatible with Google. Unlike Philips, there is no hub. Wi-fi is built into the bulb, so when it burns out, you just toss it and put another one in. It costs about $15 to $20, but will last for years.

## Switches and Plugs

If you want to turn on and off lamps that plugin without putting a smart light in it, one option is to buy smart switches. The Wemo Mini Smart Plug cost about $30 and can be controlled by the Google Home Hub.

You can plug anything into it--coffee makers, chargers--whatever you want to control remotely.

## Locks

When it comes to locks, there aren't a lot of options. It's a growing space and more options are popping up. Right now, one of the best options for Google is the August Smart Lock.

The lock is a little bulky, but it works well. Installation is the same as any other deadbolt. If you can do that yourself, then you can do this. It currently costs a little more than $250, but the company does a lot of promotions--especially during holidays.

## Sous Vide

If your Google Home Hub is going in the kitchen, then there's a good chance you'll be using it for cooking. If that's true, then one device worth checking out is the Anova Precision Cooker.

With this device, you can cook precision cook your food. Through the app, you just say what your cooking and it sets all the times and temperatures. It costs about $150.

My wife and I started using a similar device (the Mellow sous vide), which, unfortunately, isn't Google compatible, and we've saved a bundle by not going out to eat as much. I highly recommend this type of cooking!

## Doorbells and Cameras

Ring is one of the leaders in the Smart doorbell space; unfortunately, Ring is an Amazon company, and it doesn't work on Google Home Hub at this writing; the same is true with most cameras. If you want a security camera, the best option right now is Nest.